WITHDRAWN

W9-ACL-564

WITHDRAWN

DEFINITION OF A WATERFALL

JOHN ORMOND

DEFINITION OF
A WATERFALL

London
OXFORD UNIVERSITY PRESS
NEW YORK   TORONTO
1973

CARL A. RUDISILL LIBRARY
LENOIR RHYNE COLLEGE

Oxford University Press, Ely House, London W1

GLASGOW NEW YORK TORONTO MELBOURNE WELLINGTON
CAPE TOWN IBADAN NAIROBI DAR ES SALAAM LUSAKA ADDIS ABABA
DELHI BOMBAY CALCUTTA MADRAS KARACHI LAHORE DACCA
KUALA LUMPUR SINGAPORE HONG KONG TOKYO

ISBN 0 19 211830 7

© *Oxford University Press* 1973

*All rights reserved. No part of this publication may be reproduced,
stored in a retrieval system, or transmitted, in any form or by any means,
electronic, mechanical, photocopying, recording or otherwise, without
the prior permission of Oxford University Press*

*This book is sold subject to the condition that it shall not, by way of
trade or otherwise, be lent, re-sold, hired out, or otherwise circulated
without the publisher's prior consent in any form of binding or cover
other than that in which it is published and without a similar condition
including this condition being imposed on the subsequent purchaser.*

821.914
Or sd
92084
9rb. 1975

*Printed in Great Britain
by The Bowering Press, Plymouth*

for Glenys

ACKNOWLEDGEMENTS

are due to Christopher Davies, Llandybie, Wales, for permission
to reprint certain poems from my book *Requiem and Celebration*;
and to the following publications in which most of the other poems
first appeared
*Poetry Wales, Poetry Review, New Statesman,
Transatlantic Review, Planet, Aquarius, Outposts,
Anglo-Welsh Review, Second Aeon*;
Corgi *Modern Poets in Focus 5*
New Poems 1971–72, and *1972–73* (P. E. N: Hutchinson)
Poems '69, Poems '70, Poems '71 and *'72* (Gwasg Gomer)
The Best Poems of 1969, 1971 and 1972 of the Borestone Mountain
    Poetry Awards (California)
The Poetry Year (Sphere Books).
Some of the poems in this book have also been broadcast in the
radio and television services of the BBC.

CONTENTS

MY DUSTY KINSFOLK

My dusty kinsfolk in the hill
Screwed up in elm, when you were dead
We tucked you though your hands were still
In the best blanket from your bed
As though you dozed and might in stirring
Push off some light shroud you were wearing.

We did it against double cold,
Cold of your deaths and our own.
We placed you where a vein of coal
Can still be seen when graves are open.
The Dunvant seam spreads fingers in
The churchyard under Penybryn.

And so you lie, my fellow villagers,
In ones and twos and families
Dead behind Ebenezer. Jamjars
Carry flowers for you, but the trees
Put down their roots to you as surely as
Your breath was not, and was, and was.

Early and lately dead, each one
Of you haunts me. Continue
To tenant the air where I walk in the sun
Beyond the shadow of yew.
I speak these words to you, my kin
And friends, in requiem and celebration.

MY GRANDFATHER AND HIS APPLE-TREE

Life sometimes held such sweetness for him
As to engender guilt. From the night vein he'd come,
From working in water wrestling the coal,
Up the pit slant. Every morning hit him
Like a journey of trams between the eyes;
A wild and drinking farmboy sobered by love
Of a miller's daughter and a whitewashed cottage
Suddenly to pay rent for. So he'd left the farm
For dark under the fields six days a week
With mandrel and shovel and different stalls.
All light was beckoning. Soon his hands
Untangled a brown garden into neat greens.

There was an apple-tree he limed, made sturdy;
The fruit was sweet and crisp upon the tongue
Until it budded temptation in his mouth.
Now he had given up whistling on Sundays,
Attended prayer-meetings, added a concordance
To his wedding Bible and ten children
To the village population. He nudged the line,
Clean-pinafored and collared, glazed with soap,
Every seventh day of rest in Ebenezer;
Shaved on a Saturday night to escape the devil.

The sweetness of the apples worried him.
He took a branch of cooker from a neighbour
When he became a deacon, wanting
The best of both his worlds. Clay from the colliery
He thumbed about the bole one afternoon
Grafting the sour to sweetness, bound up
The bleeding white of junction with broad strips
Of working flannel-shirt and belly-bands

To join the two in union. For a time
After the wound healed the sweetness held,
The balance tilted towards an old delight.

But in the time that I remember him
(His wife had long since died, I never saw her)
The sour half took over. Every single apple
Grew—across twenty Augusts—bitter as wormwood.
He'd sit under the box-tree, his pink gums
(Between the white moustache and goatee beard)
Grinding thin slices that his jack-knife cut,
Sucking for sweetness vainly. It had gone,
Gone. I heard him mutter
Quiet Welsh oaths as he spat the gall-juice
Into the seeding onion-bed, watched him toss
The big core into the spreading nettles.

ORGANIST

Sole village master of the yellowing manual,
And market gardener: his sense of perfect pitch
Took in the cracks between the keys.
He was equipped to hear the tiny discord struck
By any weed which innocently mistook
His garden for a place to grow in.

Five days a week John Owen dug and planted,
Potted and weeded, worried
About Saturday's price in Swansea Market
For his green co-productions with God.

Walking to town at dawn, five miles
With Mary Ann his wife fluting beside him
(She, as they said, would laugh at her own shadow)
With creaking baskets laden, he nearly deafened
Himself with the noise of his own boots.

Sabbath inside the spade-sharp starch
Of his crippling collar he husbanded
On the harmonium aged couplers
And celestes into a grave, reluctant
Order; took no heed in the hymns
Of the congregation trailing a phrase behind,
Being intent and lost in the absolute beat.

But, with the years, philosopher as he was,
A Benthamite of music, he set more store
By the greatest harmony of the greatest number.
When, pentecostal, guilts were flung away
Fortissimo from pinnacles of fervour,
When all were cleansed of sin in wild

Inaccurate crescendoes of Calvary,
Uncaring, born again, dazzled by diadems
In words of a Jerusalem beyond their lives,
The choristers would stray from the safe fold
Of the true notes. John Owen would transpose
By half a tone in the middle of the hymn
To disguise the collective error,
But sure of the keys of his own kingdom.

He lies long since in counterpoint
With a few stones of earth; is beyond any doubt
The one angel of the village cloud
Who sings from old notation;
The only gardener there whose cocked ear
Can discern the transgression, the trespass
Of a weed into the holy fields,
If there are weeds in heaven.

When the moon was full (my uncle said)
Lunatic Johnny Randall read
The Scriptures in the dead of night
Not in bed by candlelight
But in the field in the silver glow
Across the lane from Howells Row;
And not to himself but to the sheep
With the village barely fallen asleep
And colliers who'd worked two-till-ten
In no fit shape to shout *Amen*
Grumbled *The bugger's off again.*

He'd dip in Chronicles and Kings
Dig into Micah, Obadiah,
Lamentations, Jeremiah,
Ezekiel, Daniel, on and on
Into the Song of Solomon:
A great insomniac heaven-sent
Digest of the Old Testament,
Faltering only in his loud
Recital when a pagan cloud
Darkened the Christian moon and bright
Star congregation of the night.

Then Johnny Randall in a vexed
Improvisation of the text
Would fill in with a few begats
Of Moabs and Jehoshaphats
(Windows banged shut like rifle-shots)
And Azels, Azrikans and all
The genealogy of Saul,

Till David's line put out new shoots
That never sprang from royal roots
And wombs long-barren issued at
The angel seed of Johnny's shouts.

When clouds veered off the moon's clean rim,
Another chapter. Then a hymn
To close the service. So he'd sing

In the big deeps and troughs of sin
No one lifts up my drowning head
Except my bridegroom Jesus Christ
Who on the Cross was crucified . . .

Then silence. Benediction: *May*
The Love of God and
The Fellowship of the Holy Spirit
Be with you always
Till the great white moon comes again.

Stillness. Until at last
Johnny would rouse himself
And take up collection from the cows.

A good fat sheep, unsheared, could have bolted
Between Will Bando's legs. They made such a hoop,
Clipping his hips to the ground,
I thought he'd been a jockey. He had the gait,
The boy's body. He strutted with careful
Nonchalance, past the five village shops
We somehow called The Square, on the outside
Edges of his hand-stitched boots, punishing
The bracket of his thigh with a stripped twig.
But he'd have slipped round on a horse
Like a loose saddle-band.

                    In fact, he'd been a tailor;
From boyhood sat so long cross-legged,
Picking, re-picking his needle as though piercing
Points of dust, his sewing hand conducting
The diminishing slow movement of silko into seam,
That his legs bent and stayed bent. His years were spent
Coaxing smooth drapes for praying shoulders
Humbled on soft-named farms, stitching Sunday-best
For the small Atlases who, six days every week,
Held up the owners' world in the colliery's
Wet headings. His box-pleats in black serge adorned
The preacher proffering the great reward.

Will Bando ate perpetual cold meat
At his life's table: doomed bachelor, burdened
With thirst as might have burned his natural
Good grace; though drink increased his courtesy.
He'd tip his hat twice to the same lady,
Apologize to walls he fell against,
Pat on the head short bushes that he brushed by.

The needle's eye of village approbation
Was wide to this certain thread. But drunk,
On a dark night, his welcome was a door locked
Early against him by his lank and grudging sister.
He'd doss down in the woodshed on clean sticks.

One Sunday, deep in the thrust of red weather
Wounding October, Will was in no rick or woodshed
We could find. He'd strayed before. But Monday came
And our feet snagged paths in the morning cambric
Of frost on field after field. Every hedge and dingle
Beaten, every crony questioned, gave echoes back
As answers. Days drifted him away. In vain we cried
Into the last derelict barn, hamlets, hills distant.
The evening paper in the market town
Printed our picture silently shouting;
And one of Will from an old snapshot with a stranger's
Smile badly re-touched to a false line.

                    Children at fox and hounds found him.
He lay in the broken air-shaft, twenty years disused,
Of the shut and festering pit, not half a mile
From home. Rubble and tumbled bricks
Gave him his sanctuary. Fallen where an unended
Dream of shelter brought him, he had given death
'Good evening'. His hat with orange feather
At the brim was in his hand. He wore his smart
Fawn herring-bone with the saddle-stitch lapels.

AT HIS FATHER'S GRAVE

Here lies a shoe-maker whose knife and hammer
Fell idle at the height of summer,
Who was not missed so much as when the rain
Of winter brought him back to mind again.

He was no preacher but his working text
Was *See all dry this winter and the next.*
Stand still. Remember his two hands, his laugh,
His craftsmanship. They are his epitaph.

AFTER A DEATH

Come back to the house, I turn the key in the door,
Pull back the curtains to let out the dark,
Kindle a fire, wind up my grandfather's clock,
Then see the slug's trail on the kitchen floor.

I have inherited him with all the rest
Of whatever's here, the pictures, the jugs, the beds
Nobody sleeps in any more. Presumably he feeds
On something here. He wouldn't come for dust.

The tables and chairs are mine, the brass trinket-box,
White plates that write their O's across the dresser,
The coats and shoes in cupboards, the old letters,
The pots, the pans, the towels, the knives and forks,

The small effects of other people's lives,
—And him who wasn't mentioned in the will,
Who entered from the garden once and still
From time to time inspects his territory then leaves.

A list's a list and offers me no order,
I see the silver trail, know other presences.
A death's a death. I mourn three absences.
If I wait here they'll speak when time is older.

THE KEY

Its teeth worked doubtfully
At the worn wards of the lock,
Argued half-heartedly
With the lock's fixed dotage.
Between them they deferred decision.
One would persist, the other
Not relent. That lock and key
Were old when Linus Yale
Himself was born. Theirs
Was an ageless argument.

The key was as long as my hand,
The ring of it the size
Of a girl's bangle. The bit
Was inches square. A grandiose key
Fit for a castle, yet our terraced
House was two rooms up, two down;
Flung there by sullen pit-owners
In a spasm of petulance, discovering
That colliers could not live
On the bare Welsh mountain:

Like any other house in the domino
Row, except that our door
Was nearly always on the latch.
Most people just walked in, with
'Anybody home?' in greeting
To the kitchen. This room
Saw paths of generations cross;
This was the place to which we all came
Back to talk by the oven, on the white
Bench. This was the home patch.

And so, if we went out, we hid
The key—though the whole village
Knew where it was—under a stone
By the front door. We lifted up
The stone, deposited the key
Neatly into its own shape
In the damp earth. There, with liquid
Metal, we could have cast,
Using that master mould,
Another key, had we had need of it.

Sometimes we'd dip a sea-gull's
Feather in oil, corkscrew it
Far into the keyhole to ease
The acrimony there. The feather, askew
In the lock, would spray black
Droplets of oil on the threshold
And dandruff of feather-barb.
The deep armoreal stiffness, tensed
Against us, stayed. We'd put away
The oil, scrub down the front step.

The others have gone for the long
Night away. The evidence of grass
Re-growing insists on it. This time
I come back to dispose of what there is.
The knack's still with me. I plunge home
The key's great stem, insinuate
Something that was myself between
The two old litigants. The key
Engages and the bolt gives to me
Some walls enclosing furniture.

THE HALL OF CYNDDYLAN

after the Welsh of Llywarch Hên: 9th Century

Cynddylan's hall is dark to-night,
No fire and no bed.
I weep alone, cannot be comforted.

Cynddylan's hall is all in dark to-night,
No fire, no candle-flame:
Whose love, but love of God, can keep me sane?

Cynddylan's hall is dark to-night,
No fire, no gleam of light.
Grief for Cynddylan leaves me desolate.

Cynddylan's hall, its roof is charred and dark,
Such sparkling company sheltered here.
Woe betide him whose whole lot is despair.

Cynddylan's hall, the face of beauty fallen,
He's in his grave who yesterday stood tall.
With him alive no stone fell from the wall.

Cynddylan's hall, forsaken then to-night,
So snatched from his possession.
Death take me so and show me some compassion.

Cynddylan's hall, no safety here to-night,
On Hytwyth's high expanse
No lord, no soldiery, no defence.

Cynddylan's hall is dark to-night,
No fire and no music.
My tears carve out their ravage on my cheeks.

Cynddylan's hall is dark to-night,
No fire, the company's all gone.
My tears tumble down upon its ruin.

Cynddylan's hall, to see it pierces me,
No fire, roof open to the sky:
My lord is dead and here, alive, am I.

Cynddylan's hall, burned to the very ground,
After such comradeship,
Elfan, Cynddylan, Caeawc, all asleep.

Cynddylan's hall, anguish is here to-night.
Once it was held in honour:
Dead are the men and girls who kept it so.

Cynddylan's hall, too much to bear to-night,
Its chieftain lost, O
Merciful God, what can I do?

Cynddylan's hall, the roof is charred and dark
Because the Englishry wreaked havoc on
The pasture-land of Elfan and Cynddylan.

Cynddylan's hall is dark to-night,
I mourn Cyndrwynyn's line,
Cynon, Gwiawn and Gwyn.

Cynddylan's hall, my open wound,
After the bustle, all the mirth
I knew upon this hearth.

CATHEDRAL BUILDERS

They climbed on sketchy ladders towards God,
With winch and pulley hoisted hewn rock into heaven,
Inhabited sky with hammers, defied gravity,
Deified stone, took up God's house to meet Him,

And came down to their suppers and small beer;
Every night slept, lay with their smelly wives,
Quarrelled and cuffed the children, lied,
Spat, sang, were happy or unhappy,

And every day took to the ladders again;
Impeded the rights of way of another summer's
Swallows, grew greyer, shakier, became less inclined
To fix a neighbour's roof of a fine evening,

Saw naves sprout arches, clerestories soar,
Cursed the loud fancy glaziers for their luck,
Somehow escaped the plague, got rheumatism,
Decided it was time to give it up,

To leave the spire to others; stood in the crowd
Well back from the vestments at the consecration,
Envied the fat bishop his warm boots,
Cocked up a squint eye and said, 'I bloody did that.'

DESIGN FOR A TOMB

Dwell in this stone who once was tenant of flesh.
Alas, lady, the phantasmagoria is over,
Your smile must come to terms with dark for ever.

Carved emblems, puff-cheeked cherubs and full vines
Buoy up your white memorial in the chapel,
Weightlessly over you who welcomed a little weight.

Lie unprotesting who often lay in the dark,
Once trembling switchback lady keep your stillness
Lest marble crack, ornate devices tumble.

Old melodies were loth to leave your limbs.
Love's deft reluctances where many murmured delight
Lost all their gay glissandi, grew thin and spare

Between a few faint notes. Your bright fever
Turned towards cold, echoed remembered sweets.
Those who for years easily climbed to your casement

Left by the bare front hall. Lust grown respectable
Waltzed slow knight's moves under the portico,
Crabbed in a black gown. You were carried out

Feet first, on your back, still, over the broad chequers.
So set up slender piers, maidenhair stone
Like green fern springing again between ivory oaks,

The four main pillars to your canopy;
And underneath it, up near the cornices,
Let in small fenestrations to catch the light.

It still chinks, spy-holing the bent laurel
With worn footholds outside your bedroom window
Through which you'd hear an early gardener's hoe

Chivvy the weeds edging the gravel path
Only to turn back into your lover's arms,
Fumblingly to doze, calling the morning false.

Lady-lust, so arranged in ornamental bed,
Baring your teeth for the first apple of heaven,
Juices and sap still run. Sleep well-remembered.

TO A NUN
after the 15th Century Welsh

Please God, forsake your water and dry bread
And fling the bitter cress you eat aside.
Put by your rosary. In Mary's name
Leave chanting creeds to mildewing monks in Rome.
Spring is at work in woodlands bright with sun;
Springtime's not made for living like a nun.
Your faith, my fairest lady, your religion
Show but a single face of love's medallion.
Slip on this ring and this green gown, these laces;
The wood is furnitured with resting-places.
Hide in the birch-tree's shade—upon your knees
Murmur the mass of cuckoos, litanies
Of spring's green foliage. There's no sacrilege
If we find heaven here against the hedge.
Remember Ovid's book and Ovid's truth:
There's such a thing as having too much faith.
Let us discover the shapes, the earthly signs
Of our true selves, our souls, among the vines.
For surely God and all his saints above,
High in their other heaven, pardon love.

IN SEPTEMBER

Again the golden month, still
Favourite, is renewed;
Once more I'd wind it in a ring
About your finger, pledge myself
Again, my love, my shelter,
My good roof over me,
My strong wall against winter.

Be bread upon my table still
And red wine in my glass; be fire
Upon my hearth. Continue,
My true storm door, continue
To be sweet lock to my key;
Be wife to me, remain
The soft silk on my bed.

Be morning to my pillow,
Multiply my joy. Be my rare coin
For counting, my luck, my
Granary, my promising fair
Sky, my star, the meaning
Of my journey. Be, this year too,
My twelve months long desire.

CERTAIN QUESTIONS FOR MONSIEUR RENOIR

Did you then celebrate
That grave discovered blue
With salt thrown on a fire
In honour of all blues?

I mean the dress of La Parisienne
(Humanly on the verge of the ceramic),
Blue of Delft, dream summary of blues,
Centre-piece of a fateful exhibition;

Whose dress-maker and, for that matter,
Stays-maker the critics scorned;
Who every day receives her visitors
In my country where the hard slate is blue.

She has been dead now nearly a century
Who wears that blue of smoke curling
Beyond a kiln, and blue of gentians,
Blue of lazurite, turquoise hauled

Over the blue waves, blue water, from Mount Sinai;
Clematis blue: she, Madame Henriot,
Whose papers fall to pieces in the files
In the vaults of the Registrar General.

Did you see in her garment the King of Illyria
Naming his person's flower in self-love?
And in the folds, part of polyphony
Of all colour, thunder blue,

Blue of blue slipper-clay, blue
Of the blue albatross? Blue sometimes

Without edge, blue liquified
By distance? Or did they start

Those ribbons at her wrists in blue
Of a sea-starwort? Or in verdigris, perhaps,
Blue on a Roman bead? Or in that regal blue
Of the Phœnicians, of boiled whelks;

That humbly-begun but conquering blue
Which, glowing, makes a god of man?
She who is always poised between appointments
For flirtation, what nuances of blue

Her bodice had, this blue you made
For your amusement, painter of fans and porcelain,
You set on gaiety; who saw, in the blue fog
Of the city, a candle burning blue

(Not heralding a death but) harbouring
A clear illusion, blue spot on the young salmon,
A greater blue in shadow; blue's calm
Insistence on a sense. Not for you

Indigo blue, or blue of mummy's cloth
Or the cold unction of mercury's blue ointment,
But the elect blue of love in constancy,
Blue, true blue; blue gage, blue plum,

Blue fibrils of a form, roundness
Absorbed by light, quintessence
Of blue beautiful. It was not blue
Tainted, taunted by dark. Confirm it.

The eyes are bells to blue
Inanimate pigment set alight
By gazing which was passionate.
So what is midnight to this midinette?

Ultramarine, deep-water blue?
Part of a pain and darkness never felt?
Assyrian crystal? Clouded blue malachite?

Blue of a blue dawn trusting light.

SUMMER MIST

Branches have common tenancy
Arrangements, moving in and out
Of one another's air at the wind's
Say-so. Where their top joints belong
Is never clear-cut:

Except as when hiatus calm of August
Forestalls September. Then mist
The silencer happens into grey,
Mist variously impaled upon the land
Subtracts the pulse of colour.

On such a windless day two men, their
Voices ravelling its few hours, gave
And gave way in words. Easily
They could have sung together.
They knew each other's unsung tunes.

Dusk and the mist closed on them
In the last lane. Now one instructs
The other: 'Remember that the wind
Will soon return, remember
You are welcome to my air.'

POSTCARD FROM THE PAST

Among old bills in a cluttered drawer
I come upon it, wonder why I kept it.
In lese-majesty and love, the stamp's stuck
Upside-down. The postmark re-endorses
The name of the resort. Children on rubber horses
Tame the hand-tinted sea. But there is no address

Except my own—an old one—naming a place
Where I am known no longer. Stock phrases
And news of old weather send me a dead greeting.
The signature is indecipherable.
Nothing makes sense except the final X.

LETTER TO A GEOLOGIST
for Wynn Williams

When was it we last met? When the stag
Devoured the vivid serpent then wept
Jewels as tears, antidote to all poisons.

Or so it seems to me. You write
Of your November find, fossil coral
Within a spit of that house of yours

(Which is too far from me. The free hold
Of our friendship is at stake); the coral,
Bring me a piece of it, bring it soon.

I would place it with that other handful
Torn, only last year, from a living reef
Six thousand miles away in the Indian Ocean;

And, in the pairing, see what you deduce:
That once your Flintshire hill—for me as distant
As the Seychelles themselves—was tropical.

The shifting land you've shown me: off-shore
Islands in green counties; tide-ways
500 million years of age under the plough;

And desert sands stranded in river-cliffs
On Deeside, come from the Sahara.
If these could move, could not *you* move, too?

Come south. Ferns in grey shale speak of you
From my shelf, of coal measures we were both
Born on. Your nugget of fool's gold

Is paperweight over the dross of my draft poems.
I know that, as I greet you, mountains shrink
Or inch up; the sea-kings' beds are unmade;

But these are rustlings, mere cosmic sighs
Unheard beneath our breathing. Let us tell
Some part of earth's true time together soon

With a drink, a song—the lullabies you sang
My children, come sing them again before sleep;
Let us say to each other words of a common world.

I've grown too solemn, so recall your jest
Of Man's not really falling off the peg
Vertical, ready-made, in Genesis:

But should you, in the field, come upon Moses
Striding through cloud on a Snowdonian height
With new or adjusted Tablets of the Law

Please check the Lord's amendments
Before you raise your hammer to opine
What stone it is that they are carved upon.

Yours, as the mountains move,
                              Love, ever,
                                        John.

ANCIENT MONUMENTS
for Alexander Thom

They bide their time off serpentine
Green lanes, in fields, with railings
Round them and black cows; tall, pocked
And pitted stones, grey, ochre-patched
With moss, lodgings for lost spirits.

Sometimes you have to ask their
Whereabouts. A bent figure, in a hamlet
Of three houses and a barn, will point
Towards the moor. You find them there,
Aloof lean markers, erect in mud.

Long Meg, Five Kings, Nine Maidens,
Twelve Apostles: with such familiar names
We make them part of ordinary lives.
On callow pasture-land
The Shearers and The Hurlers stand.

Sometimes they keep their privacy
In public places: nameless, slender slabs
Disguised as gate-posts in a hedge; and some,
For centuries on duty as scratching-posts,
Are screened by ponies on blank uplands.

Search out the farthest ones, slog on
Through bog, bracken, bramble: arrive
At short granite footings in a plan
Vaguely elliptical, alignments sunk
In turf strewn with sheep's droppings;

And wonder whether it was this shrunk place
The guide-book meant, or whether
Over the next ridge the real chamber,

Accurate by the stars, begins its secret
At once to those who find it.

Turn and look back. You'll see horizons
Much like the ones that they saw,
The tomb-builders, milleniums ago;
The channel scutched by rain, the same old
Sediment of dusk, winter returning.

Dolerite, porphyry, gabbro fired
At the earth's young heart: how those men
Handled them. Set on back-breaking
Geometry, the symmetries of solstice,
What they awaited we, too, still await.

Looking for something else, I came once
To a cromlech in a field of barley.
Whoever farmed that field had true
Priorities. He sowed good grain
To the tomb's doorstep. No path

Led to the ancient death. The capstone,
Set like a cauldron on three legs,
Was marooned by the swimming crop.
A gust and the cromlech floated,
Motionless at time's moorings.

Hissing dry sibilance, chafing
Loquacious thrust of seed
This way and that, in time and out
Of it, would have capsized
The tomb. It stayed becalmed.

The bearded foam, rummaged
By wind from the westerly sea-track,
Broke short not over it. Skirted
By squalls of that year's harvest,
That tomb belonged in that field.

The racing barley, erratically-bleached
Bronze, cross-hatched with gold
And yellow, did not stop short its tide
In deference. It was the barley's
World. Some monuments move.

WINTER RITE

Mother-of-pearl in cloud, the sun low
Over the holy island; the straggle
Of sacred timber flexed and crook-back
For the dark months' long assailment;
And the lake where the god sprawls
Sleeping under rotted water-lilies, weed
Clogged at his groin.
      Safe fish weave basketries
Of bubbles through his fingers.
Year in, year out, in this wan season
We bring him offerings: spears, axes,
Sickle-blades, bronze scoops and bridle-bits.

We have given him prisoners
For his drowned army, their screams at the knife
Sleep-songs for his still warriorship.
He is a god, he knows our service.

We have taken the great boar live
Then cast it into his pool, fenced it
With sacrificial arrows. It threshed
Until it died for his fresh food.

Year after year before the god's lake freezes
We climb to his stone altars. They tilt
Above the lilies which were gold in summer.
We face, despite our fears,
The god's invisible three faces.
      We do not expect to see him.
He allows us to approach and accepts our gifts
With the silence of all gods.

TRICEPHALOS

The first face spoke: Under sheep-run
And mole-mound and stifling glade
I was awake though trapped in the mask

Of dirt. Counting the centuries,
I scrutinized the void, but its question
Stared me out. What was it I remembered

As, above me in the world, generation
Upon futile generation of tall trees,
Forest after forest, grew and fell?

It was that once the ease, the lease
Of a true spring saw my brow decked
With sprigs, my gaze complete and sensual.

My eyes (the second said) were fixed
In hunger for the whole regard
Of what might be, the god beyond the god.

Time and again the black loam blazed
And shuddered with false auguries.
Passionless, vigilant, I kept faith,

Invented systems, sounds, philosophies
In which some far, long-listened-for,
Long-perfect melody might thrive.

The imagined dropped away, the perfect
Knew no advent. My sight was lost in sleep
And the stone sleep was haunted.

Two living garlands (spoke the third)
Strove to be one inside our common skull.
They half-entwined the unavailing dreams

Fashioned from light that is and words
That seemed ours for the saying.
I await wisdomwise enough to know

It will not come. The inaccessible song
Upon whose resolution we, awake, expectant,
Yearning for order, lie, is the one tune

That we were born for. Its cadence
Shapes our vision and our blindness.
The unaccountable is my stone smile.

LAZARUS

Finally (in this dream) the Roman
Thrust his sword right through me.
I woke upon a pain which would not go.

It would be futile to describe the days
That followed, to talk of flame and fever,
Of red-hot irons and the like:

I was on fire with pain. I bore it badly.
They gave me cordials of blue-flowering
Borage but the fever would not break.

The last time I came round the pain had gone:
Then, after the long night, at dawn
The window blurred back into darkness.

I know you would have me tell you
Of spirits standing in white groves to meet me,
Of staircases ascending to the skies,

But that I cannot do. I have grown old
With the bandage-marks still on me.
They show me what I was and what I will be.

As you go home you will think, 'Death's secret
Was not his because he was not destined
Yet to be dead.' I cannot say.

I only knew of nothing and that, too,
Was of the world. I limp in the sun
Knowing that other. Darkness has its right.

His cry that ripped me out of nothing
By my roots, calling my name, that brought me
Back to the spectre of the light,

That cry, I hear it still in sleep.
I come awake, but paralysed, my arms
Imprisoned in the sheet, my legs rigid,

Unshivering cold. Sleep-walkers move
Without waking. I wake and cannot move.
How long this lasts again I cannot tell you,

A moment or an hour. It passes when I hear
Voices, long silent, in the courtyard saying,
As once they did, 'Lazarus, yes, Lazarus.'

SALMON

first for, and now in memory of, Ceri Richards

The river sucks them home.
The lost past claims them.
   Beyond the headland
It gropes into the channel
Of the nameless sea.
   Off-shore they submit
To the cast, to the taste of it.
It releases them from salt,
Their thousand miles in odyssey
For spawning. It rehearsed their return
   From the beginning; now
   It clenches them like a fist.

The echo of once being here
Possesses and inclines them.
   Caught in the embrace
Of nothing that is not now,
Riding in with the tide-race,
   Not by their care,
Not by any will they know,
They turn fast to the caress
Of their only course. Sea-hazards done,
They ache towards the one world
   From which their secret
   Sprang, perpetuate

More than themselves, the ritual
Claim of the river, pointed
   Towards rut, tracing
Their passion out. Weeping philosopher,
They reaffirm the world,
   The stars by which they ran,

Now this precise place holds them
Again. They reach the churning wall
Of the brute waterfall which shed
Them young from its cauldron pool.
   A hundred times
   They lunge and strike

Against the hurdles of the rock;
Though hammering water
   Beats them back
Still their desire will not break.
They flourish, whip and kick,
   Tensile for their truth's
Sake, give to the miracle
Of their treadmill leaping
The illusion of the natural.
The present in torrential flow
   Nurtures its own
   Long undertow:

They work it, strike and streak again,
Filaments in suspense.
   The lost past shoots them
Into flight, out of their element,
In bright transilient sickle-blades
   Of light; until upon
The instant's height of their inheritance
They chance in descant over the loud
Diapasons of flood, jack out of reach
And snatch of clawing water,
   Stretch and soar
   Into easy rapids

Beyond, into half-haven, jounce over
Shelves upstream; and know no question
   But, pressed by their cold blood,
Glance through the known maze.
They unravel the thread to source
   To die at their ancestry's
Last knot, knowing no question.
They meet under hazel trees,
Are chosen, and so mate. In shallows as
The stream slides clear yet shirred
   With broken surface where
   Stones trap the creamy stars

Of air, she scoops at gravel with fine
Thrust of her exact blind tail;
   At last her lust
Gapes in a gush on her stone nest
And his held, squanderous peak
   Shudders his final hunger
On her milk; seed laid on seed
In spunk of liquid silk.
So in exhausted saraband their slack
Convulsions wind and wend galactic
   Seed in seed, a found
   World without end.

The circle's set, proportion
Stands complete, and,
   Ready for death,
Haggard they hang in aftermath
Abundance, ripe for the world's
   Rich night, the spear.

Why does this fasting fish
So haunt me? Gautama, was it this
You saw from river-bank
At Uruvela? Was this
   Your glimpse
   Of holy law?

DEFINITION OF A WATERFALL

Not stitched to air or water but to both
A veil hangs broken in concealing truth

And flies in vague exactitude, a dove
Born diving between rivers out of love

In drums' crescendo beat its waters grow
Conceding thunder's pianissimo

Transfixing ancient time and legend where
A future ghost streams in the present air:

From ledge to pool breakneck across rocks
Wild calm, calm chaos skein their paradox

So that excited poise is fiercely dressed
In a long instant's constant flow of rest,

So that this bridegroom and his bride in white
Parting together headlong reunite

Among her trailing braids. The inconstancy
Is reconciled to fall, falls and falls free

SAYING

Andiamo amigo. We think we see
What we would say. But we lie
Prisoners within those words
We happen to know, captives behind
Bars of arbitrary sound. We grind
Meaning to a halt at the cell wall.

Language, vocabulary, are not the jail
But sounds made ugug, ciphers
That lock one meaning in and exclude
All others. So we express
Exclusive interim reports, construct
A rough equation in makeshift
Habitual sound. We tap on the jail's
Waterpipes, signal through stone
And wait for the vague answer.

So if I say *Areft paradenthic slodan
Aberra antelist mirt maroda*
You say that I say nothing. Though perhaps
I name the god of all green vines;
Or name that process which makes wine
Cloud in the cellar when spring sap climbs
In its far vineyard, but name it
In an inconvenient language not invented,
Or invented once and lost
And now forgotten.

CARL A. RUDISILL LIBRARY
LENOIR RHYNE COLLEGE

LAMENT FOR A LEG

Near the yew tree under which the body of Dafydd ap Gwilym is buried in Strata Florida, Cardiganshire, there stands a stone with the following inscription: 'The left leg and part of the thigh of Henry Hughes, Cooper, was cut off and interr'd here, June 18, 1756'. Later the rest of Henry Hughes set off across the Atlantic in search of better fortune.

A short service, to be sure,
With scarcely half a hymn they held,
Over my lost limb, suitable curtailment.
Out-of-tune notes a crow cawed
By the yew tree, and me,
My stump still tourniqued,
Awkward on my new crutch,
Being snatched towards the snack
Of a funeral feast they made.
With seldom a dry eye, for laughter,
They jostled me over the ale
I'd cut the casks for, and the mead.
'Catch me falling under a coach',
Every voice jested, save mine,
Henry Hughes, cooper. A tasteless caper!
Soon with my only, my best, foot forward
I fled, quiet, to far America:

Where, with my two tried hands, I plied
My trade and, true, in time made good
Though grieving for Pontrhydfendigaid.
Sometimes, all at once, in my tall cups,
I'd cry in *hiraeth* for my remembered thigh
Left by the grand yew in Ystrad Fflur's
Bare ground, near the good bard.

Strangers, astonished at my high
Beer-flush, would stare, not guessing,
Above the bar-board, that I, of the starry eye,
Had one foot in the grave; thinking me,
No doubt, a drunken dolt in whom a whim
Warmed to madness, not knowing a tease
Of a Welsh worm was tickling my distant toes.

'So I bequeath my leg', I'd say and sigh,
Baffling them, 'my unexiled part, to Dafydd
The pure poet who, whole, lies near and far
From me, still pining for Morfudd's heart',
Giving him, generous to a fault
With what was no more mine to give,
Out of that curt plot, my quarter grave,
Good help, I hope. What will the great God say
At Dafydd's wild-kicking -climbing extra leg,
Jammed hard in heaven's white doorway
(I'll limp unnimble round the narrow back)
Come the quick trumpet of the Judgement Day?

THE BIRTH OF VENUS AT ABERYSTWYTH

Beyond the pier varicose waves crocheted
A complex permanent nothing on the stones.
The Corporation deck-chairs flapped
Haphazard unison. Most sea-front windows

Confessed to Vacancies; and on the promenade
A violinist in Scotch-plaid dinner-jacket
Contributed little to the Welsh way of life
As he played 'Thanks for the Memory'

To two small children and a dog. Without
Any expectation at all, the sea brandished
Its vanity. The one-eyed coastguard was dozing.
Nothing in the sky sought a response.

The occasional pebble moved, gave itself back
To the perpetual, casual disorder
Of all perfectly-shaped, meaningless forms,
Like pebbles. There was one beachcomber,

From Basingstoke, but he noticed nothing
Unusual either when far out, beyond
The beginning of the ninth (one could even
Go as far as to say the ninetieth) wave,

Dolphins who hadn't spoken to each other
For years formed squadrons for her.
Trenches of water broke open, deep
Where she was, coming up. Weeds fandangoed,

Currents changed their course. Inside
An instant's calm her hair began to float,

Marbling the hollows like old ledgers.
The sea still tells the story in its own

Proud language, but few understand it;
And, as you may imagine, the beauty of it is lost
In the best translations available . . .
Her different world was added to the world

As, nearing shore, sensing something dubious,
Something fishy in the offing, the dolphin-fleet
Turned back. The lady nearly drowned,
But hobbled in, grazing her great toe.

Do not ask questions about where she came from
Or what she was, or what colour was her hair;
Though there are reasons for supposing
That, when it dried, its light took over

Where the summer left off. The following Sunday
She wore a safe beige hat for morning service
At the Baptist Church. Even so, the minister
Ignored her as she left, and she didn't go again.

PARAPHRASE FOR
EDWIN ARLINGTON ROBINSON

It was Sod's Law and not the sun
That made things come unstuck for Icarus.

The same applies to all with a seeming head
For heights, a taste for the high wires,

Flatulent aerialists who burped
At the critical moment then fell akimbo

In a tattered arc, screaming, down
Out of the illusion, the feathery Eden.

So when your mother died of black diphtheria
And neither quack nor priest would call

To give their pince-nezed ministrations,
You and your brothers wrung cold compressess

In vain for her wild brow, cleft her grave
Yourselves, thumped clods on her plank coffin.

Later one brother took to drink and drugs.
The other slotted the family investments

Into curt bankruptcy. Meanwhile your father
Tried coaxing ghosts. Table-tappings

Stuttered perniciously from the next room
To yours, harangued your shuttering deafness.

Sometimes you imagined you detected clues
To a code, but it was only the singing wires

Of the death of the aural, the eighth nerve
Shrinking from lack of blood. That fenced you

High on a dangerous peak of vertigo, giddy
But unfalling. You said you mourned a 'lost

Imperial music'. What you were emperor of
Was a domain you did not recognize

As worth the name: a kingdom of aspirers
Without wings, a thin parish of prophets

Without words—except for baffled Amen,
A scraggy choir without a common hymn,

But no man without music in the throng
And each man sawing at his own bleak tune.

THE PIANO TUNER

Every six months his white stick brings him,
Punctilious to the minim stroke of nine
On the day we dread. Edgy at his knock,
We infuse a grudging warmth into voices
Asking his health, which courtesy he refuses;

And usher him to the instrument. He entrusts
Us with nothing, disdains, from his black tent,
Our extended hands where the awkward staircase
Bends, rattles the banisters with his bag,
Crabs past the chairs. Finally at the keyboard
He discharges quick arpeggios of judgement.

'As I expected,' he says, dismissing us;
And before we close the door excludes us
Further, intent in his flummox of strange tools
And a language beyond us. He begins to adjust
And insist on the quotients and ratios
Of order in encased reverberant wire.

All morning, then, downstairs we cower;
The thin thunder of decibels, octaves slowly
Made absolute, which will not break into storm,
Dividing us from him. The house is not the same
Until long after he leaves, having made one thing
Perfect. 'Now play,' say his starched eyes.